TO THE DISAPPEARANCE

Todd Fuller

MONGREL EMPIRE PRESS
NORMAN, OKLAHOMA, UNITED STATES OF AMERICA

2015

FIRST EDITION, 2015

To the Disappearance
© 2015 by Todd Fuller

ISBN 978-0-9903204-6-3

Except for fair use in reviews and/or scholarly considerations, no part of this book may be reproduced, performed, recorded, or otherwise transmitted without the written consent of the author and the permission of the publisher.

Cover Art
Sending Her Prayer to Everyone She Loves
©Sonny Howell, 2015

"Buffalo Skulls" photo is a public domain image shared by Wikimedia Commons

MONGREL EMPIRE PRESS
NORMAN, OK

ONLINE CATALOGUE: WWW.MONGRELEMPIRE.ORG
This publisher is a proud member of

COUNCIL OF LITERARY MAGAZINES & PRESSES
www.clmp.org

Book Design: Mongrel Empire Press using iWork Pages

CONTENTS:

Coming and / or Going	1
Out of the Stars: Meanwhile, the Sky Is a Cultural Text	3
Infrastructures:	4
To the Museum of Endangered Sounds: a Community Collaborative	9
The Unusual: in Oklahoma	14
Off Frame / In Frame	18
A Late-Night, Re-Broadcast of The Buffalo Shooting Championship of the World: (with Pre- and Post-Game Commentary)	20
The Usual	29
Vanishing Cream: the Animator's Confession	32
To the Disappearance:	36
To the Flip-Flops (which belong to a Man) Left at a Park alongside a Picnic Table:	39
In Perpetuity: and Other Disappearancesb in 7 Parts	41
Outline of a City Brushed in Colors of Poignant Crescendos	49
A Cremation Story & Other Jazz by Jorge Sandoval	51
Giving Memory an Address	55
Tobacco & Coffee	57
(Or Dying at the Window)	63
An Index of First Lines:	65
Notes to the Collection	67

Acknowledgements

I would like to thank a number of friends (readers, editors, teachers, and acquaintances) who provided feedback, insights, suggestions, and encouragement along the way. They include: Bruce Bond, Co-Workers at the Center for Research Program Development and Enrichment (CRPDE), Monique Ferrell, Stuart "Sy" Hoahwah, Geary Hobson, Randi LeClair, Lisa Lewis, Wilma Mankiller, Simon Ortiz, Cecil Sayre, Tony Spicer, and Gabe Wingfield.

I am also grateful to family and friends who encouraged me: Cherye and Dave, all those in Indiana (the Fullers, McClouds, Blacks, Kadingers, Bishops, and Wards), and the Howell family in Pawnee and elsewhere in Oklahoma; also to Little Buddy, Jaxon, Jimmy, and Sidney: *Iriwe turahe*.

The following pieces were first published, sometimes in slightly different versions, in the journals listed below:

"An Index of First Lines," *Apalachee Review*

"Off Frame / In Frame," *Barnwood Magazine*

"Coming and / or Going," *Cimarron Review*

"Tobacco & Coffee," *Cimarron Review*

"Outline of a City Brushed in Colors of Poignant Crescendos," *New York Quarterly*

"The Unusual (in Oklahoma)," *Poet Lore*

"Giving Memory an Address," *Red Earth Review*

"Out of the Stars: Meanwhile the Sky Is a Cultural Text," *Red Earth Review*

"The Usual," *Third Coast*

"A Late-Night, Re-Broadcast of The Buffalo Shooting Championship of the World: (with Pre- and Post-Game Commentary)" *Halvord Johnson's Truck* <http://halvard-johnson.blogspot.com/2015/04/i35-creativity-corridor-todd-fuller.html>.

"To the Disappearance," *Wicazo Sa Review*

To my wife, Randi, and our two children, Eli and Teagan. Forever—

To the Disappearance

When one tugs at a single
thing in nature, [one] finds it
attached to the rest of the world.

—John Muir

I seem to be defying fate; or am I avoiding it?

—Frank O'Hara

Some Meditations

Coming and / or Going

The planet groans every time
it registers another birth
　　　　　　—Paul Simon

: The earth / bends / on its axis. And so
You have (at this moment) taken your place
Inside the revolving door.

: Meanwhile, complicated / aeronautical /
Circumstances push the moth to its implosion
Against a murderous, yet unassuming, sedan.

: (Within the enclosed space of paper and
Thought, that which you think / and type /
Could [just as easily] be newly sewn raven's

Wings echoing / or breathing / against
Borders, or something to that effect).

: And a son is born / with new mixtures
/ Or equations / of blood that irritate, ignite,
And, of course, enflame old colonial scars.

: And a holy man is interred / (because holy
Men [and Women] still roam from one bruise,
Or / purpose / to another) among the masses.

: This is every new life sliding / swimming /
Flying / & hatching its way into the (blinding,
Ever intoxicating) revolution.

: Conversely, this very hour will be the only
One of its kind with each of its / ridiculous
/ Seconds vanishing against your active or

: Inactive palms. / And so, we are all coming
And / or going at a pace that belongs to some
Kind of astronomy / with its fluid (& ancient)

: Rotation. / Here in Oklahoma (the Indian /
One) a brown body is snuffed of its life / with
The all-too-eager snap of a trigger / and ?s

: (Of course) remain lingering on barroom
Air & smoke & fist-to-cuffs for generations
To come. / Perhaps you are terrified

: Of crossing bridges / or vast spaces / or,
Maybe turning in circles makes you weak
/ In the knees—not like when you spun in

: Abandon, twenty years ago. Since then,
The list of those expired stretches from / you
To the end of your recollections. Likewise,

: The list of those learning to negotiate an
Erection and (their own) breasts extends
From hand to hand and beyond their lips.

: And so, here we are (the 7 billion) stuck
In the door (and all in the same neighbor-
Hood) while balancing nickels on our

: (Ashy) elbows. Everyday: It's coffins and
Cradles. / Out of the womb and / or into
The ground. / Otherwise, you and I are

(Momentarily)

: Caught in the middle: between two / worlds
& The possibility of your next / precisely
Calculated / glance. And what we all / see

: Next / the taking and leaving of first and
Last breaths / is the precise equation of our
(Adding and subtracting) flesh.

Out of the Stars:
Meanwhile, the Sky Is a Cultural Text
—on the occasion of July 13*

And all those constellations running
Free after nightfall.

All those celestial connect-the-dots.

And who among us hasn't hung their
Gods on the stars?

Even tonight, Van Gogh's Moonrise is
A returning goddess.*

Even tonight, my astronomical weakness
Is ancestral.

And taking flight is an un-earthly
Meditation on faith.

All those jets bisecting the universe
Into a vast checkerboard.

And all those satellites feeding us
Constant intelligence.

Meanwhile, down here against
The terrain, any moment or touch could
Well burst into flames.

Infrastructures:

        i

There's a carnival in every heart,
And electricity runs it all.

There's an ocean in the blood,
And sometimes you crave both
Salt and beach. So it seems,

Lines, ubiquitous lines, run every-
Where (below an earthly surface)
And the body is no different.

Take, for instance, the story of

A man in Alabama who removed
His ruptured appendix with a butter
Knife and pint of whiskey.

He later told his folks that the ghost
Of Bear Bryant* provided him
The strength necessary

To endure.

ii

Now, I'm sure the sun too is
An author: beams composing
One blossom after another.

Even through kitchen blinds,
I watched sunlight write
In perfect English.

(And what to make of
"HI" Across the floor?)

I had no choice but to retrieve
The camera and create a sacred
Story for the kids.

iii

Meanwhile, our sons & daughters
Keep dying in accidents,

And the litany of perpetual eulogies
Is astounding.

Meanwhile, a teacher in Michigan
Gives birth to sextuplets,

And (altruistic) corporate donations
Arrive from afar, even

As the bidding war escalates for rights
To the inevitable reality show.

iv

There, under your feet,
There, over your head,
There, inside the walls,

There, along the road,
There, whether seen or
Unseen, are utilities

Feeding the Nation.

And so, here's a cup of coffee.
Here's popcorn and a movie.
Here's a warm shower and
The toilet with its reliable

Flush.

Here's to the pilot light
And ensuing entrée.
Here's to clean laundry.

Here's to engineers and architects.
Here's to the hands that guide
The tape measure and drill.

v

Out beyond suburban strip-
Malls and multiplexes,

Out beyond rows of car
Dealerships and fast-food
(chains),

A countryside remains.

Beyond layers of asphalt
And building pads,

Beyond railroad lines
And ocean crossings,

Beyond hardhats
And batter boards,

The landscape contracts
To a postage stamp.

And sunlight has no word
For the disappearance
Of earth.

To the Museum of Endangered Sounds:
a Community Collaborative

T. Fuller[1] S. Howell[2] C. Clark[3] M. Korhonen[4] A. Quick[5] N. Miller[6] A. (Ward) McCloud[7] R. LeClair-Fuller[8] E. (Zachary) Ludwig[9] T. Petersen[10] L. (Spurgeon) Kent[11] J. Ried-Yund[12] E.S. Fulman[13] G. Wingfield[14]

From my memory: I have long forgotten the sound / of my great grandmother's voice / but I remember her fear of storms / a fear that created thunder along each / nerve to my stomach. / I remember her heavy black shoes / climbing down stairs and her stockings / drooping (also in fear) to her ankles. // Everything shook in her body / including her thoughts, which must've darted / from her long-deceased husband to / her rhubarb (along her sidewalk garden / and which she used to make the best / pie in Montgomery County). She'd / ask me how it tasted, / and I'm sure I said sour / strawberries, or something like that—and twisted my face into disdain. / Somehow, I think her garden spoke the ancient / language of seeds and sun / earth and water.[2]

From my wife's uncle on Facebook: Some days, I want to be a biologist / who studies the bird calls of extinct species / in China. Then, other days / I feel old-timey urges to / walk to Nebraska (our homeland) and listen / to Sandhill Crane migration patterns. // I remember how my dad used to whistle tunes. / I wondered what part of joy lived / inside him to make such sounds. // And then I heard a story about his service / in the Korean War—how he wrapped soldiers' / wounds with Pawnee songs. They would ask, / "Where'd that come from?" / And he'd tell them, "Ancient places—good places—that didn't / have war." // Then, on other days, I'd see him walking down the street / silent as (~~extinction~~) that first moment after a song disappears.[3]

From co-workers: Bells, of course—all types of bells: cowbells / the ringing of cash registers—those old NCR's / telephones /

clocks (before digital alarm clocks) / and church bells—god, church bells every day / and bell towers and town bells / school bells and dinner bells—all those bells bringing us / together. / And I still recall my gran'pa—God rest his soul—hanging off the porch / his right arm shaking / with that dinner bell moving this way and that. // Once he made it to the table, / he'd wheeze all over us. But he did manage / to say Amen after the prayer. And then / tell one of us kids to pass gran'ma's Prize-winning chicken. // Not long after that, his breathing became an extinct sound.[4/5]

From cousins: What is the sound of a sunset without / pollution? And what sounds emanate from / a withered typewriter ribbon? / Surely, the human heartbeat will be / an endangered sound someday. What about / campfire cultures and popping embers? What of / bubbling percolations from an old coffee pot, / whirring machines that sew, rattling / radiator heaters, pump organs, whistling / teapots that penetrate tenement walls? The clopping of horses walking on brick-paved roads. Sometimes / silence is the most endangered sound.[6/7/8]

From my wife: Love makes no sound. We see / only expressions, manifestations, and echoes—none / of which serve as accurate representations. // For me, the popping of bacon / in a cast iron skillet / is not endangered. Neither is / Charlie Pride's voice pouring out of a radio. But / the tapping of my gramma's feet / (to all of it on a Saturday morning) is. / Her kitchen ambiance (in 1988) radiated / while her hum-along to "Kiss an Angel Good Morning" / made rooms glow. / It feels like endangered tastes and smells.[9]

From a girl who was / is my friend in high school in Indiana: Something about all of it (gravel popping / under tires on a Sunday afternoon / windows rolled down during an early Fall sing-along / to the Rolling Stones' "Satisfaction" / and Dairy

Queen ice cream dripping off our chins / with Dad yelling "don't make a mess!" / as cigarette smoke burst through his mustache / while we dreamt of Walter Payton's perfect / smile* and let out a chorus of "no-no-no!") feels / long gone.[10]

From a patron at Abner's Ale House in Norman, Oklahoma (after going on his 3rd then 4th beers): Well, the sweet wail of a Patsy Cline concert, for one. / And I suppose my great uncle's wooden / screen door slamming shut on a 4th of July evening / or ice clanking against a glass pitcher / full of lemonade. Damn. // And all the crickets—all in unison—singing their leg / rubbing songs out in pecan groves. And surely, the clang / of our childhood voices is an extinction, not endangerment.[14]

From a we've-got-nothing-better-to-do, so-let's-get-phds-in-creative-writing-and-literary-criticism friend: Music, anything music related, and the changes in technology that have allowed devices to become more personal: First it was the single live performance; then albums and the scratch of records and the way needles popped when you first set the arm on the vinyl; then 8-tracks, which you could carry with you and play in your car; then cassettes came along, and they'd whirr and squeal to a stop —always startling; now CDs and MP3s and iPods—I mean you can carry your own jukebox in your pocket. // And, okay, then there's the moment on August 18, 1969, when Jimi broke into the "Star Spangled Banner,"—an epoch sound—which was also the song of my first day in the world.[11]

From an entomologist buddy in Indiana: Running your summer finger / along a bedtime window screen / while the whirr of a metal fan / accompanies cicada clicks, you hear / your sister's boy-crazy voice (under a 19th century oak tree), / which carries each syllable as if future lives / and civilizations hang in the balance. The girls sharing / the streetlight circle with her / speak as if / talking required no breath. They are surrounded by / a swarm of gnats, and their conversation plays / like a see-saw back & forth between Greg and gnats. Meanwhile, / in the room next to me, I hear the stumbles / of my older brother who likes to mix / combinations of PBR and doobies. He talks / to himself about Sarah and Jenny and says / he can't decide, so mopes in his room—eyes bloodshot / with a future full of Vietnam. In an hour, he will be asleep when / mom-n-dad romp through the front door / only to tumble into the kitchen and devour leftover chicken / and peas. After, they slur-yell about / That got'dang Johnson / [Bobby] Kennedy and King. / And how I didn't go to Korea / to fight for this America. All / these moments—part of my (Saturday / night) aural heritage. Flies (musca / domestica) scrambling all over the windowsill / with their songs of entrapment.[12/13]

From a cultural economist: how about real money in your wallet or / pocket? How about the various sounds (noises) associated with / higher education? Real labs replaced by virtual ones. / Real campus malls replaced by virtual tours. / Real jobs replaced by declining job market projections (for recent college graduates). / Reasonable college debt replaced by inflated debt. / So, how about the empowerment of education / as an endangered sound? How about would-be engineers / poets / chemists / sociologists / biologists / and philosophers / eschewing college because of the cost? / What is the sound of an academic / discipline or profession gasping for its future? / And then there's the climate, which is certainly / an endangered being.[14]

From a musician and former bartender who is an encyclopedia of the hip and obscure: Of course you would expect me to say something like / the dialing sound of a rotary phone, so I'll go / with whistle pops and cast-iron doorstops. / I'll go with the snap of the first bottle tops. / I'll consider the voices of those born in 1924 / including Lauren Bacall—who knew a thing or two / about whistling and telephones. / And I'll go with the clicking sounds of TV / remote controls—Zenith Space Commanders / from the 1960s, which makes perfect sense (in my James T. Kirk dreams).[15]

From a book collector: The smell of old books is an endangered / perception. Back in '49 Dad opened / the Poet's Pause (on 2nd & Main) and soon employed / the services of "Pushkin," a Russian Blue / for the predictable purpose of double entendre. Forty years / later, he left the store to me and wished me / luck. He said (before he left) that gratitude is / an endangered hope. Now, I believe Daumier's *Man / Reading* in a Garden captures a disappearing / lifestyle.[14]

From a socio-audiologist's notebook: Aren't endangered sounds really just temporal judgments of memory—relative to: 1/the recaller's memory, 2/the era during which they lived, 3/available technology, and 4/personal relationships? // We all have specific variables that create personal sonic maps, / which means our aural histories are all over the words we use / and stories we tell. / It's how we create our personal auditory pathway. And all / around us—whether rural or urban, coastal or inland, Indigenous or immigrant, natural or synthetic, nocturnal or diurnal—the world / resonates emphatically.[14]

From an ethno-musicologist: Nostalgia will never be / an endangered sound.[14]

The Unusual:
in Oklahoma

The left hand of time
paints my hair gray,

and farmers come to town
to steal the spot of noon.

They cast shadows over
their chicken-fried steak

lunches, and the bills
of their baseball caps

have been finely curved
into half circles. I've

learned that conception
is the first frontier. It's got

something to do with
exact temperatures

and a meiotic twirling of
chromosomes. Perhaps

it's all genetic memory—
the way an ancient drop

of blood makes forced
entry into my thoughts;

the way most mammalian
hearts come with a billion

beat guarantee. Soon
I will leave Mary's Grill

and return to my desk
where I can begin to consider

the circumference

of Walt Whitman's waist.
And when the farmers
make ready to leave,

they will prop themselves
against their pickup trucks

and talk in half-
hour soliloquies.

As a small boy I remember
large men watching football

on tv, and their words
came out something like: You

stupid idiot, and
What a dumb ass,

as they spat a stream
of vehement damns, shits,

and hells at the black
and white screen.

And perhaps it's all social
nurturing—hours listening

to lemon drops
dissolve in my mouth,

minutes watching a black
widow spin a web in the corner

of the garage, and the orange
hourglass on her belly

shimmering like some hypnotic
Egyptian dance.
And maybe the color of dust
is a way of life.

Maybe zero is a sacred
place holder in the word

behold. Maybe
there's a calico cat named

Jenny scampering across
Charles Darwin's backyard

at Down House. And maybe
the lexicon of the circle

will finally destroy
all boundaries.

One day I'll open the paper
and find that the Washington

R*dsk*ns drafted the memory
of Jim Thorpe.

I could split open right now
and discover five European

tribes; declare myself colonized
once and for all.

When I return to Mary's
for dinner I see

the same men eating
chicken-fried steak entrées

with their wives.
And their conversation

centers on grandchildren
instead of football,

and eventually they
give a howdy to all

twenty people eating
in the room. They're

lifetime residents, and they
miss their children who've

moved to Chicago, or Florida,
or Oklahoma City.

Sooner or later I'll return home
with hand-picked images

of my breath, and then I'll have
every angle of light memorized.

Off Frame / In Frame
—to RLC

Language is the blood of thought,
And so the sun sets alongside two
Crows. And beside them two men
Who belong to a moonlight town.
Their eyes are rivers and sighs—as
If the past were flowing into every
Moment. And soon the birds take
Flight to finish their songs. Soon
Enough the moon's mouth is one
Blushing serenade. The unmowed
Grass is a chorus. The tall blades
Say "Shhhhhhhh/Shhhhhhhh" over
& over. At some point, the daydream
Continues: & out in the distance
There's a blue tent beside the water.
Curiosity allows us to see two dark-
Haired figures scurry inside. They
Won't emerge for a few more hours.
When they do, it's all sticky smiles.
And the man leaves a sweaty pool
In a woman's bellybutton and his
Tongue swims for redemption. This
Is one way that love begins. There
Are a million others. It could start
With glances meeting across some
Vast room, or with whiffs of perfume
Dangling five feet above a sidewalk.
No matter, at some point it always
Whirls through the imagination, and
When it does, you allow yourself to
Believe. And surely, that echo of
Childhood laughter can't be too far
Removed from the tap in your feet.
Surely, we haven't given up on King
Or Yeats or Petalasharo.* Somehow
We might yet find the heart nothing
But a thick-petaled flower wilting
Toward Jerusalem. And what to make

Of water's reflection at your feet and
The perfect sound of snapshots falling
From your hands? And if you could
Orchestrate beauty for one day, how
Would you begin? What diseases,
Deceit, or heartache would you first
Delete? What would God / Buddha /
Allah make of a day without rescues?
And somewhere across the expanse,
Dawn is cracking out of its shell with
Another explosion.

A Late-Night, Re-Broadcast of The Buffalo Shooting Championship of the World:
(with Pre- and Post-Game Commentary)
   —*After L. Frank Baum*[1]

Pre-game / Preface:

One day, one typically quiet day in my Intro to Native American Studies course (at the University of Oklahoma), we discussed an article by David D. Smits (College of New Jersey) titled, "The Frontier Army and the Destruction of the Buffalo: 1865-1883." What follows is the culmination of an exercise that initially occurred after our discussion. I am grateful to the class for their willing participation. (The post-game notes are intended to be an interactive piece.)

———

1880 /
It's a shiny-bullet shine
On a sun-drenched day
That covers horizon to
Horizon.

Providentially blue skies
Wash the bucolic plains
Of Pawnee, Oklahoma.

Multitudes of men and
Beast populate the scene
Near Pawnee, Oklahoma.

This afternoon, Sherman[2]
And Sheridan—heroes
Of Civil War fame—meet
On thunderous fields.

Sides have been chosen—
Grand dukes and princes
On one, CEOs and

Railroad barons on the
Other.

Meanwhile, soldiers and
Trappers await their daily
Sport @ 3 bucks a hide
And .25c per tongue.

And soon enough, Buffalo
Bill will engage his rifle—
Signaling the event's
Commencement.

Soon enough, shots will
Volley from yonder railcar,
And cloven-footed beasts
Will scatter.

Naturally, Sheridan's boys
Take an early lead—ghosts
Of Custer's 7th firing with
Ethereal precision.

Across the way, Teddy
Roosevelt's eyeglasses and
Mustache brandish swords
From every obtuse angle.[3]

Hooves and gunshot shake
The hills as special guests
From Russia ask about
The aborigines:

Which means Sherman will
Deny his middle name and
Chew cigars into (Crazy
Horse's) bones while

Dropping the biggest bull
With his tintype stare.[4]

(It means the pink bosom
Of *Manifest Destiny* in one
Hand and a copy of *The
Wizard of Oz* in the other.)[5]

Across the field, Hitler's
Future imagination peeks
Into reservations and
Fills with prophetic
Sketches.[6]

At halftime, the score is
Tied at a 1000 skins
A piece, even as herds
Of Natives skulk toward
D.C. and starvation.

(Somewhere on the upper
East side [about 59th and
Madison], a woman named
Helen drinks tea in her
Sitting room.

While other women
Are busy making idle
Gossip, she imagines
Herself

Undressed and arching
On the buffalo hide
Below her feet.

She hears the
"Iroquois Galop"[7]
[In her head]

And sees herself
[Naked and]
Writhing with
A smile.)

When the two sides re-
Commence, the field
Has already soaked up
The bloody evidence—

Carcasses shoved aside.
Turkey vultures circle
In biblical halos above
Smoke clouds.

And Mt. Rushmore is
The perfect American
Prayer (even as Indiana

Boys consider the sacred
Physiologies of bison
Lungs at 100 bullets
A minute).

Bystanders applaud
In leather gloves,
Discuss theoretical
Possibilities of
Quivira.[8]

Elsewhere, Albert
Einstein's Hopi war
Bonnet takes down 10
Cows per feather,[9] and

After 6 hours, there is no
Last shot to win it at sunset;
No 9th inning heroics.

Next to the horizon,
The score is a single
Stack of skulls—as
High and wide as a new
Two-story town.[10]

———

Post-game / Notes

[1] L. Frank Baum (1856-1919) is best known as the author of the beloved children's story, *The Wonderful Wizard of Oz*, which was published in 1900. Though originally from New York, Baum and his wife, Maud (Gage) Baum, moved to Aberdeen, Dakota Territory, in the late 1880s and opened a general store. After his store failed, Baum turned to newspaper writing for The *Aberdeen Saturday Pioneer*. On December 20, 1890, Baum wrote of Sitting Bull's murder, which occurred on December 15, and declared, "The Whites by law of conquest . . . are masters of the American continent, and the best safety of the frontier settlements will be secured by the total annihilation of the few remaining Indians." He continues by stating, ". . . . Their glory has fled, their spirit broken, their manhood effaced; better that they die than live the miserable wretches that they are. . . . We cannot honestly regret their extirmination [sic] . . . ." Then, the in January 3, 1891 edition of his column, he stated: ". . . Having wronged them for centuries, we had better, in order to protect our civilization, follow it up by one more wrong and wipe these untamed and untamable creatures from the face of the earth."

In 2006, descendants of Baum went to the Pine Ridge Reservation and offered a formal apology to the Lakota Nation for the role that their forbearer played in the Wounded Knee Massacre, which took place December 29, 1890.

[2] The quote, "The only good Indian is a dead Indian," is attributed to Sheridan. However, multiple sources indicate that Sheridan told Comanche chief, Tosawi, (at a Fort Cobb conference in 1869 with 50 other American Indian representatives), that "the only good Indians I ever saw were dead." This was after Tosawi suggested to Sheridan that he was a good person, a good Indian.

[3] In 1886 TR said: "I don't go so far as to think that the only good Indians are dead Indians [in reference to Sheridan's often misstated quotation], but I believe nine out of ten are, and I shouldn't like to inquire too closely into the case of the tenth." He also stated that, "The most vicious cowboy has more moral principle than the average Indian. . . . The Indians are . . . [r]eckless, revengeful, fiendishly cruel, they rob and murder . . . defenseless, lone settlers on the plains." A New Yorker born into privilege, Roosevelt completely adhered to notions of racial superiority and manifest destiny—a prisoner of eugenics and myopia, like so many during his time.

[4] General Sherman's full name was William Tecumseh Sherman (1820-1891). He was named for the Shawnee chief with whom his father "caught a fancy," at least according to Sherman's memoir. Family and friends referred to him as "Cump." Sherman is perhaps best known for his march across the U.S. south during the Civil War. His

lack of respect or compassion for any race (or cause) other than his own is well-documented.

[5] *Manifest Destiny*, (aka *American Progress)*: a canvas painted by John Gast (in 1872) in which he depicts a female representation of the United States—and all her European / non-Indian "frontier, settlers"—spreading westward over a broad prairie. Also depicted are Indians, buffalo, and other "wild critters" fleeing US expansionism. (Note: the U.S. government could have, at any point during its history, declared that westward expansion would cease. In fact, notions of U.S. expansion / colonization continue to the present day. The Euro-American drive to own one's own property / land / house is one that remains to this day—often cloaked [in part] in a notion that morphed into an idea known as "The American Dream.")

[6] Hitler's admiration of the U.S. government's genocidal policies toward American Indian nations is fairly well documented and even hinted at in *Mein Kampf*—especially in V1, ch 11. Further, Hitler biographer John Toland noted in his 1991 book, Adolf Hitler: "Hitler's concept of concentration camps as well as the practicality of genocide owed much, so he claimed, to his studies of English and United States history. He admired the camps for Boer prisoners in South Africa and for the Indians in the Wild West; and he often praised to his inner circle the efficiency of America's extermination—by starvation and uneven combat—of the red savages who could not be tamed by captivity" (702).

[7] The "Iroquois Galop" was a popular 1880s song written by an individual calling him- / herself, "Le Baron." The publisher of the music was C.H. Ditson & Company, a significant publisher of music (in the U.S.) from the 1780s to the 1930s. Attempts to identify the composer's specific identity have been unsuccessful, as the following link demonstrates: http://imslp.org/wiki/Category:Le_Baron. Such a song title suggestions typical post-colonization romanticizing of items / activities associated with American Indians—especially those who have been conquered or have perished.

[8] Quivira refers to a Native North American town (settled, most likely, by the Wichita tribe) first mentioned by Francisco Coronado in 1541 and which is believed to be located in central Kansas. The backstory is as follows: Coronado led an expedition north from present-day Mexico in search of the "seven cities of gold." He soon encountered the Hopi, some Pueblo towns, and the Zuni, who were settled in adobe towns with small farms. Once the tribes learned of Coronado's motive, they told him stories about a place to the north and east (on the Great Plains) where people lived in golden houses and drank from gold cups, which hung from the tress. An Indian, known as The Turk, led Coronado and his troops across the panhandle of Texas and into Kansas in search of Quivira. However, upon encountering other

Natives, Coronado was convinced that the Turk was deliberately misleading the group. According to some, it is believed that the Turk, who was possibly Pawnee, hoped that the group would get lost in the vastness of the Plains. In the end, Coronado found a Wichita town with about 25 dwellings (grass-thatched houses) but no golden cities. For his role, the Turk was executed by strangulation.

[9] In 1931, Albert Einstein and his wife were inducted into the Hopi Tribe as honorary members. The professor, who was being courted by administrators at Cal Tech at the time of the photo, stood with members of the Hopi nation. The Hopi reservation is about 100 miles from the canyon. Also, the Hopi did not wear such headdresses, and they did not practice any pipe ceremonies.

[10] (See photo preceding notes.) In numerous descriptions of this photo, different bloggers / scholars state that the buffalo skulls shown in the photo are to be ground into fertilizer. Truth is, this image is most disturbing (to me) because of the vastness of death, greed, and land lust (colonization) that is both implicitly and explicitly depicted. One perpetrator of the slaughter of buffalo in Oklahoma and elsewhere included William Matthew "Bill" Tilghman (1854—1924), who claimed to have killed more than 1000 animals—starting when he was fifteen. Later, he became a major law enforcement figure in Kansas and Oklahoma; he also served as a state senator and as sheriff in Cromwell, Oklahoma, where he was murdered at the age of 70. Tilghman's murderer was Wiley Lynn, a corrupt Prohibition agent, who was later killed by agent Crockett Long of the Oklahoma State Crime Bureau.

The Usual

                    i

More than a hundred million
T.V. sets will light the universe
Tonight, and the miraculous

Glow will slip, like a feather,
Between lovers' bodies. I'd like
To believe we evolved from birds,

That love's wingspan reaches
Beyond the four flimsy branches
Of the heart. And even though

Astronomers will chart another
Pulsar today, teenagers will be
Masturbating across the country;

Morticians will remain active
In every county. And those twins
Of history, cock and cunt, will

Continue to elude extinction. I'd
Like to believe that the sun will
Unravel one beam at a time,

That reptiles (at obtuse angles)
Will expose themselves on red-
Baked stones: that someday

I'll be true to my heliotropic
Tendencies and follow the path
Of daylight across my yard.

ii

Just once I'd like to say beautiful
Without people rolling their eyes.
Because tonight at Dora's Diner

We'll have pre-frozen burgers
And eighty-four cable channels
For everyone's eating and viewing

Pleasure, and the soft hypnotism
Of black and white movies will
Confound the landscape of grand-

Parents and divorcés. Just once
I'd like a headline that reads
"Chicago Cubs Win The World

Series"—for once, a moment
Of silence to be observed all day:
A contemplation of my own

Christmas day murders, and
How I was sent out, after presents
Were opened, to a mouse-infested

Garage with orders to kill. Now
I'm beginning to empathize
With the moment a language

Evaporates, the way words
Disappear into graceful obscurity,
How mindfuls of memory spill

Into stainless steel sinks.

iii

When I crawl into bed tonight
I will be dazzled by crisp sheets.
And the ringing of my day will

Reverberate from my ears into
My feet, and I will twitch into
Wakefulness. I'm beginning to

Scrutinize the necessity of
Refrigerator magnets, how so many
Of life's significant reminders

Hang alongside photos of infants
And clippings of cartoon strips.
I'm beginning to question

The aesthetics of daylight-saving time,
To doubt those ancient paradigms of
The seed, plow, and hands of time.

I have memorized the profiles
Of cardinals in cautious postures
At the bird feeder and am convinced

Of the magical powers of their
Curved tongues. So what if
I've quit waking near my dreams?

I've memorized the future
As revealed in the palm
Of my hand.

Vanishing Cream:
The Animator's Confession

I'll admit it—to sitting
At my desk for hours
On end and re-imaging
Revisions in fantastic
Realms. (This is the way
My father lived his life:
Always opining over the
Dream that got away;
The half-brush with
Financial security that
Alluded him; always a tech
Stock in which he would
Have invested—if not
For the new baby on the
Way. This is the tone
That permeated his pre-
Dementia tirades.) I'll
Admit to the same what-
If-ing condition—and I am
Certain that somewhere
There must be a metaphor
That cures all physical
And metaphysical ailments:
That some days we desire
To disappear beautifully
At will, one cell at a time,
Molecule by molecule, or
To vanish or make others
Go away—all discomforts
Resolved, all nincompoops
Dissolved. Eventually,

You realize there's nothing

Wrong with the world
That cartoons can't fix.
You're never surprised
When Foghorn Leghorn

Or Jerry (the Mouse) or
Yosemite Sam applies
A thick coat of Miracle
Vanish, & before you know
It: a chair levitates / a bat
Swings / a string pulls /
An enemy squelched—it's
All morals & justice. Just
Once, where is the chance
To dissolve through walls,
To hear a conversation
(Among the "deciders"),
To sneak in undetected
At world premiers and
Farewell concerts, to eaves-
Drop on the solemnity of
Sacred sites? O, to be a
Momentary ghost slipping
Between shades & time,
To balance a razorblade
On each eyelid, when we
Really want miracles in
A jar—all that time dis-
Appearing from facial
Corners, as if there were
Angles living in mirrors.

Some Protests

To the Disappearance:
—after the Poet Ai

Call me the great
Colonizer, the one
Who conquers with
Abandon and Bible
Armed with sword
& ideology. Watch
Me on the feather of
An Angel's wing. I
Have seen ancient
Tongues disappear
With a woman's last
Breath. I have seen
Ways of classifying
The world dissolve
With a man's final
Heartbeat. I have
Calculated salvation
One heathen and acre
At a time. Watch me
Divide the land into
Perfect squares, cut
The continent in half
With silver railroad
Lines. With this, I
Have cut the skins of
Buffalo off their hides
And watched the red
Man whither on his
Weak horse. His drum
Nearly quiet, his flute
Nearly broken. I am
The bullet and flame
That destroys silence.
I am the holy massacre
That pierces a child's
Eyes. I am the wool
Blanket that incubates
Infection. I am all of

This in the name of pro-
Gress. I am your forced
Removal and forced
Assimilation. I am your
Negotiated treaty with
An "X." I am your
Bottle of spirits known
As manipulation. I am
Your headmaster at all
The boarding schools,
Poised to strike with
The ruler and unfazed
By your rehearsed tears.
I am the recorder of
Black and white photos
And wax cylinders.
I have divvied up the
Land in allotments &
Called it yours. I have
Been certain of your
Farming future. I follow
You on your powwow
Highway and see your
Bald tires. I follow your
Children to school and
Nurture moments of self-
Doubt. I am the creator
Of political turmoil &
Kakistocracies* all across
Indian Country. I weave
Perpetual stereotypes
Of the buckskin and tipi.
I listen to your 49 songs—
Recognize the yearning
In your voice. I hear
The Hey-ya, yearning
In your voice. I know

You sing with your eyes
Closed. You sing in
Languages that have
Started slipping into
Mist. One breath at a
Time, you sing until
Your heart bursts into
Memory.

To the Flip-Flops (which belong to a Man) Left at a Park alongside a Picnic Table:

I want to believe it was love (lust even)
That compelled a man to forget / leave /
Abandon his shoes on a hot summer
Day (in Norman, Oklahoma). I want
To be convinced that the attraction
Was too much—that lovers gazed (for the
First time, perhaps) into one another
And could no longer cage / control /
        contain
Their emotions. I want to believe they
Rushed to the car and began hurried
Movements that accompany untapped
        passion.
(I do not, however, want to imagine
The all-too-predictable writhing / thrusting /
Gyrating of body parts as they practiced
The sexual arts.)

I want to imagine that it might have
Been an unintended oversight—that
Maybe he returned later to find
Them in exactly the same spot. That's what
I want to believe. I don't want to
Imagine anything nefarious /
Dastardly / or underhanded—nothing
Unusual. I don't want to read some
Bottom-of-the-page missing person's story
On the local media's webpage. I don't
Want to learn personal details about
"The Victim" or his family—his mom
& dad, or how they worked so hard to
Get him through college. I don't want
        to know.

I have no interest in learning facts
About his lover, where she came from (North
Dakota or wherever), or how they
Met (in a grad-level psychology
Class or wherever), or what their future
Plans might've included. Perhaps they
Headed to Vegas or Mexico for
Something impulsive. Maybe they headed
Out for adventures in Alaska, where
Such footwear would be superfluous. I,
For one, am certain that some lovers can
Vanish as quickly as courage from bodies
Sliced at the vocal chords.

IN PERPETUITY:
AND OTHER DISAPPEARANCESB IN 7 PARTS

> As long as the grass shall grow
> And the rivers shall flow*
>   —U.S. Treaties

> There is water
> at the bottom of the ocean
>   —Talking Heads

ONE: ON THE DAY OF YOUR CONCEPTION

$6 in the bank
& walking through wal-mart
again
& asking myself *condoms or
diapers*?
& walking from one section
to the other
& thinking sex or responsibility
& looking over selections
of each
& trying to find a math way
to get both
& looking at the cheapest
diapers
& wondering about the cheapest
rubbers
& hearing too many stories
about flimsy latex
& them busting in the dark
& what the hell—$6 dollars—
just enough for a 6-pack
& smokes

Two: June 23, 2013 Is a Random Day
To Teagan

This is the only time
This day will exist, and
No other like it will happen
Again. Once

It has ended, nearly 384,000
New souls will have entered
The fray, and nearly 156,000
Will have exited.

Each day disappears like
The one before it, and our
Daughters will populate
The planet

For a thousand years to
Come.

THREE: U! S! A!

A moment of silence for
The farmer,

With his antique plow and horse.

A moment of silence for
The Plains Indian,

With his dwindling buffalo herds
And land.

A moment of silence for
Ghosts, & ghost mines,

And ghastly hope
Withering in the desert.

Four: The Sears Catalog

Kit homes & the Wish Book (for
Christmas desires & tensions),
Parlor Organs & cast iron stoves,
Women's fashions from one
decade to the next & the Sears
Motor buggy (for $395.99 &
[so] Safe a child can run it, &
Flat crepe at .29 a yard, & whirling
Yards of taffeta in vibrant hues,
As well as the world's best
Royal Blue Vermont Marble
For all your headstone needs,
Alongside Smart Fashions in
Hats starting at 1.39, next to
Electric belts and jewelry ga-
Lore, baseball mitts & sewing
Machines, fine dining alcoves
For $14.95, and the 6 Million
Dollar Man action figure for
6.44. And all those Halloween
Costumes—of chicken feather
Headdresses and other NDN
Apparel—just for (high vol.)
Kicks.

Five: Every Four Years (& 1" W of the MS Riv.)

The myopia glistens like
Collection plates.

That's how it is out here
In the land of (God =

America) Red States. When
All is said and done,

(With the sunset shimmering
Like the pink heart of Jesus),

You might even find folks
Fighting, fornicating,
& laughing

Enough to convince
Themselves they
Found love.

Six: Homage to Sustainabilty

Turn off the alarm:

Piss.
Make coffee.
Check email &
Weather Report—
Chance of rain.
Take shower.
Dress, Good-bye.
Drive & arrive.
Make coffee.
Check email.
Do this/Do that.
The weight of bills
& Expectations.
Eat Lunch.
Do more. Clock
Out. Eat Dinner.
Do nothing but TV
Or read. Poems.
Fall asleep on the
Couch. Wake.
Go to bed.

Turn on the alarm.

Seven: Landscapes and Grandpas

Gravity's equation goes
Something like this:

Our forces attract one
another until we intersect.

Now, at every 4-way stop
in America it's a gas station /

Church / liquor store / and
Bank. Gone, are the corner-

Side movie houses, 5 & dime
Stores, Pontiac dealerships,

And pool halls. Once, my
Dad told this story of a man

Who owned a bar / pool hall
And who had the fellas over

For poker every Thursday.
And this one time, things

Got outta hand when the
Man (all liquored up) ran

Outta resources. So he
Went into the kitchen and

Grabbed some papers. He
Returned with the deed to

His house, slammed it on
The table and said, "By Gawd!"

This was just before someone
Else's four-of-a-kind beat his

Full house.

Outline of a City Brushed in Colors of Poignant Crescendos

Lose your dreams, and you will lose your mind.
—The Rolling Stones

Those mad scientists of metaphysics
Continue diving into ashtrays and

Conundrums. And just outside their
One-volume bookstore, a dog keeps

Breathing coffee steam. Meanwhile,
Moonlight splatters a suicide rhyme

Against the street. And magnificent
Amputations of the heart smell like

Whiskey. Across the way, guitars and
Jesus converge on a man's tongue.

The occasional passerby tosses coins
Between the musical notes without

Making eye contact. Elsewhere, people
Are procreating by the thousands at

This very moment. And young lovers
Will be tempted to proclaim their love

Too prematurely. As it is, the sky's as
Skinny as a bone, with architectural

Puzzles crowding air with steel and
Glass.

And someday you could find yourself
Eating butterfly wings with Salvador

Dali. Someday each breath will be
A memory you've taken for granted.

Sometimes it feels like there's a ghost
On every street and corner seeking

Some color of redemption. The old
Rain plays a startling song on the roof.

A Cremation Story & Other Jazz by Jorge Sandoval

In memory of my cousin, Apple Quick

I have forgotten
How to grab
Words (pesky
units of thought
& representation),
Or how to
Arrange them
Attractively.
It's like I can't
Remember how
To think or
Breathe or blink
Or drink.
It reminds me
Of the story
About Jorge
Sandoval, the
Trumpet player
From Cuba who
Lost his lips
To cancer.
The spark
Lived on,
But he had no
Way of giving it
Expression.
So he took up
The drums
(for years)
Until an accident
At the factory
Gnarled his
Hands into
Rubber knots.
All that was left
Was a voice
Made of soot

Cigarettes & dark
Shades of rum.
And songs poured
Out of his curled
Lungs until men
And girls cried.
Once the cancer
Bit into him
Again, he finalized
His affairs, took
All the necessary
Steps, including a
Post-cremation
Ceremony:
All his loved
Ones gathered by
The seaside,
A beautiful table
Set banquet-far-
And-wide with
Red snapper, rum
Cake, pan Cubano,
Frijoles negros,
Huevos habaneros,
Pork & salsa, and
Rice everywhere—
Bottles of rum at
Every other setting.
Toasts and laughter
Flowed aplenty.
His music drenched
Ears and air alike.
They ate the beans
And pork and fish,
Crinkled their
Brows with each
Taste of salsa
And eggs. "Mis

Dios," they sighed.
And their mouths
Took in the food.
Their tongues felt
And savored it.
All their throats
Willingly swallowed
Until nothing was
Left of the sun—
Until the day
Moved elsewhere.
Beforehand, Father
Perez gave offering
For the food, said
Prayers worthy of
A national hero,
Raised his hands
And eyes skyward,
And spoke from
Roman Catholic
Liturgy, "This is
My body / Eat
Of it." The next
Day, after the rum
And bread ran
Their course,
The island was
All trumpets
And drums and
Ancient dances
With women in
Dresses, daughters
Spinning in home-
Made floral prints,
Sons moving in
Comfort. And their
Words approached
Resonations that

Touched every
Delicate curve of
Hands, voice, lips.

Postscript:

Meanwhile, long
Ago, my sweetheart
Dreamed of music—
Harbored fantasies
Of smoke-filled bars
& piercing 5 minute
Guitar solos on
Her purple Ibanez,
Which she bought
Courtesy of student
Loans. She would
Talk n talk—carry
On for hours about
Making it in LA or
Seattle or Athens or
Or Tulsa. Now, our
Son / on two-year-
old legs / spins as
His mom plucks
Away on the back
Porch. He spins
And spins until he
Falls and the words
"Rock n roll baby"
Twirl out his
Mouth. His mom
And I look at one
Another—all too
Knowing glances
That equal fear. So
I begin to write.

Giving Memory an Address
> —*To H.M., who (unknowingly) sacrificed his memory to save his life (traded seizures for amnesia) and thus became an heroic character in numerous dissertations and journal articles.*

The universe is (after a blink
or 2) tinseled fabric made of
breath.

Elsewhere, the brain is its own
electric constellation full of
astral addresses

& impulses networking, one
forgettable moment to the next.

Now, my memory lives in a place
no one has seen.

And each crackle of sunrise gives
way to daily self-invention—
my name a mystery to the body
I carry around.

Likewise, down the street, I am no-
where recognizable—
with a man

who calls himself my son.
And the woman he calls his mom
resides in a moment

as fictional as starlight. That is
the way each day begins: and
these claws at the ends

of my arms are called digits,
and these talons at the ends of my
legs are toes, and

this entity at the top of my neck
contains eyes, behind which
are rooms known as the brain,

where lives memory. And they
tell me it is no where close to
the heart.

TOBACCO & COFFEE

i
America cannot begin again,
But if it could there might be
Star-spangled arrows aimed
At the Atlantic, arcing in the
Millions toward white sails.
And action-thrillers make it
Easy for us to imagine death
Expressions passing across
Some Conquistador's face.
As it is, there are times when
I equate paradise with truck
Stops in Oklahoma, where
Denim and double negatives
Adorn the landscape. A "How
Do" and tip of the cap—just
Enough romantic fare to set
A spark.

The other afternoon a crow
Dropped turkey bones at
My feet a week after Thanks-
Giving. And birds eating
Birds, the remains as gnarled
As a city sidewalk. I swear it
Sounded like laughter falling
From the sky. Now I'm sure
That sirens are stopping rush
Hour traffic somewhere: the
Equation of a cardiac arrest
Unfolding inside a sunlit
Cherokee cab; or, maybe
It's another domestic dispute
Upstairs, a well-aimed knife
To the thigh. Truth is, we
Keep on breaking each other's
Lives with great efficiency.
And each Sunday there's a
Full house in the Trucker's

Chapel, a cozy little trailer,
Just off the highway near
Tonkawa, Oklahoma.

ii
I've seen a woman reading
Romance novels by herself
In a corner booth at Denny's,
Watched two pots of coffee
Disappear down her throat.
And sometimes there's no
Consolation in a moonlit
Night. I've heard the voices
Of America's AM talk-radio
And thrown my fist into the
Steering wheel. I've listened
To lonely men contemplate
A burning cigarette, their
Baseball caps and mustaches
A common motif, confusion
And divorce shared themes.
Sometimes they live by cliché
Alone. Sometimes it's the only
Dimension of thought in the
Tri-state area. And I can hear
The myth of that mighty
American Dream stomping
Across a playground. It's all
Kids screaming for position,
Kicking on the monkey bars.

& Maybe I finally disappeared
Into a woods last weekend,
Made myself naked in a stream
Before the trees & sunshine
& God; maybe I closed my
Eyes and imagined my arms
Wrapped around someone;

Maybe I heard the stream
Reciting Neruda poems. And
At one point, I counted eight
Deer staring down at me and
Said Hello; their glances perfect
Against my body. And a part
Of me knows I should've never
Left that moment—the skin
Of the trees wrinkling
Into a precise map.

iii
On some mornings, it's like
The light of day barely breaks
My skin. And I'll wake up
Wondering whose life I'm
Living. Sometimes I can walk
Down a county road and hear
Other languages. And I'll try
To speak a few of its words,
Concoct some cozy translation
Before returning to English—
Tonight, the moon will wear
A sliver, like a silver bracelet
Barely hanging on a woman's
Wrist. And then, at some point,
We realize we've left pieces
Of our lives lingering inside
The memories of those we've
Kissed: and sometimes, I'm as
Elegiac as a whistler in a park.
And I'll blame it on Gauguin.

Somewhere across the way,
A child takes her first steps
To a room full of applauding
Relatives. And somewhere
Else, a woman's feet, wrapped

In yellow M&M boxes, take
Her last—to no one's applause.
She'll be found clutching an
Apple core in her right hand.
This is your America: I can see
All the prayers lifting skyward
In the trillions, one after the
Other like raindrops returning
To clouds. And maybe there's
A gallery of tears that hangs
In my throat. Somewhere, more
People ought to be falling in love.
There ought to be more hands
Cupping a loved one's face.
& I've learned my heart has
Its own imagination, realized
It's impossible to laugh and
Whistle at the same time.

iv
This is the mid-night snack
Crowd at Wal-mart, all eyeing
The bakery possibilities, and
Too many folks pondering
Selections in the chip aisle.
I can hear them mumbling
Prayers to the nacho and
Doughnut, half of them still
Carrying their remote control
Clickers. Once in a while I'd
Like to roam through a day
Fingering the veins of a red
Maple leaf. Maybe the only
Perfect landscape belongs to
The imagination. I've even
Discovered my face wrapped
In a pair of hands belonging
To my best intentions. I know

It's been too long since I last
Threw a glass in anger against
Some wall. In those younger
Days, my bedroom door was
Scarred with fist blows—jagged
Constellations. Sooner
Or later, every conclusion is
A façade.

If only for tonight: drops of
Moonlight pour into my eyes
& Blur time's flawed equation.
And there's no way to dodge
Regret or the scent of an orange's
Broken skin. Maybe the Pope
Will someday canonize Miles
Davis' trumpet. Right now,
I'm as ancient as my body, which
Took generations to complete,
Same as yours. & Somewhere,
Someone has said I'll never grow
So old again. And the force field
Of the heart is thin as a sheet.
I can hear the wind on these
Tree tops beginning to mimic
Oceanic voices.

v

A time lapse of love might look
Something like this: your beauty
Is your lie, America. And dawn
Is always breaking into sweat.
By now, my dreams have left
Lasting injuries. Somewhere,
I should be driving, or healing,
Or dancing, or picking out some
Tattoo, or reading another book,
Or walking away from this land,

Which never belonged to me.
It'll be another cup of coffee
And one more cigarette today.
I want to believe in the wisdom
Of swollen and purple lips that
Bloom with a night of kissing.
I want my body back, like I want
America returned to its first
Children, and women, and fathers.
And sooner or later, I'd like to
Believe in gardens, in the song
The throat wants to sing to itself.
For now, it's "road rage experts"
And pundits of the old "sudden
Wealth syndrome." It's selling
The sensational. It's your body
And mine crowding buildings,
Roads and homes, sidewalks and
Movie theaters. Somewhere else,
It's prairie, fence posts, livestock.
And somewhere else, it's nothing
Like either. Maybe someday,
(Perhaps on the count of three?)
We'll agree to look into one
Another's eyes. Maybe those
Shooting stars were arrows last
Night. And if nothing else, I
Might be lucky enough to untie
My memories and boots at the
Same time. If nothing else, there's
A place in my mind where wind
Always curves against my face.
& Now, each body is the beginning
Of a story I've been waiting to hear.

(OR DYING AT THE WINDOW)
Love / is a burning thing
—Johnny Cash & June Carter Cash

The last honeybee of the season
Limps alongside the window

: Has arrived in Pawnee / Oklahoma*
To complete its final task

With no fanfare /

Here: Where history (equals)
A tainted blanket of long
Remembrance

Constellations are arranged by
Memory / Here:

The story is (not) so parenthetic /

Elsewhere / lovers are gone —
Their caskets buried deep as a man
Is tall / and

: The windshield crumpled into
Their bodies / left shredded skin

Between each turned crease /

: Now daughters & grand daughters
Make the graveside journey to
To gaze at chiseled

Names / to talk to the deceased

In normal tones while piercing
Earth with artificial daisies / to

Recite family narratives about
"Grampa" answering the door
Grinning / and naked

Here: if I could (without injury)
I might offer the bee / some

Impression of comfort /

As it is / the moon appears as if
The only light in town and

: Corners are places where
The world becomes exact.

An Index of First Lines:

"You don't want to feel the universe in every sentence."
—Norman Mailer, NPR, 1/31/03

All that economic prattle fumbling against your hopeless pockets
And then there's always the possibility of a redemption cluttering the sky
And what of that first tentative kiss given to your lips behind the shed?
And what to do with another night of traffic-jam anthems over coffee?
And where to re-locate once those fractured words settle quietly on the couch?
Because I could forget how to ride a bike through the city park at dusk
Because traces of laughter might be echoing against windy tree tops
Before a complete stranger approaches your eyes, there is a sidewalk
Before the delicacy of black hair falls against your untouched skin
By the time another year offs itself, maybe a new lover   car   job   home
Can the distance of time be measured in glances and lost socks?
Chicanery, tomfoolery, hoopla, angst, amuck, and other shades
Cut free as a desert night and riding that black ribbon beside God's own profile
Dusty as cans of fruit cocktail on the back shelf in a Texas truck stop
Each moment—a memory of some kind drifting back to
Every face caught in the lie of a moonlight moment
Finally, a moment of grace caught in the act of picking up trash
Gyrating fans in the sanctuary and sweaty prayers stuck to the spine
He (of University Avenue fame) gathers each can as if flecks of gold leaf

Her body has forgotten those simple functions—and handfuls of dirt
His body has forgotten how to lean into his hunger for another's scent
I could cut remnants out of the sky and hang a story above the newborn
I have looked out to the ocean and wondered why we ever crawled out
I might begin today with some kind of resolve—maybe a pop tart & CNN
I would dare tickle the sun's falling light across your legs with
Just for tonight, how 'bout the suffering pleasure of Kurt Cobain?
Lonely as a trickle, she spirals into the liquor store still believing
Losing love can be like that—
Maybe, amid the torment of choices, there are other universes I could peek into
Maybe the pinch of two lives twisting into one another
Maybe two slices of bread and a sliver of mustard
Never again
O, the ragged rain falling through a streetlight's steamy radius
Perhaps those footsteps outside the door are clouds come
Quietly across the alley he discards trinkets from a former life
So what if I've quit waking near my dreams, I've seen the future
Some day I might even prop myself up with faulty memories & six-packs
Somebody will walk above your grave and your dusty bones will remember
Somewhere out in America it's layoffs and fists and predictable blood
Supple as a gorgeous sunset flashing its pink tail
There are cracks in the sidewalks and outlines of states in each one
Time, that cagey escapist, will surely yawn this morning
Under bridges, puddles and cardboard boxes, flocks of birds scattering
What to make of a stillborn heart forever silenced in its cage?

Notes to the Collection

Out of the Stars
On the occasion of July 13, 2003: the moon Van Gogh painted in his famous Moonrise made an exact spatial reappearance—so scientists at Southwest Texas State University determined after a year-long study.

Infrastructures
Paul "Bear" Bryant (1913-1983) was a legendary football coach, most notably at the University of Alabama, where he guided the Crimson Tide to six national titles. As a result of his accomplishments, he remains a celebrated figure, both in Alabama and in college football circles.

To the Museum of Endangered Sounds
Note: the idea for this piece occurred after I listened to an NPR story about a college student who put together a collection of bygone tech-related sounds: the sound of a typewriter, logging on to a 56k modem, the sound of the Pacman video game, etc. My idea for this poem sprang from the notion that some poems lend themselves to collaborative activities—to multiple voices with multiple perspectives—much in the same way that the scientific community often employs a team model to write academic articles. I used tools of social media, casual conversation (with individuals I knew), interviewed individuals in numerous settings, and so on. I allowed participants to define "endangered" in any way they chose. What follows is a truly a collaborative creative effort. I thank all who participated and acknowledge them with a writing credit. (Please note: several of the sections are purely fictional; in such cases, I have either: 1) provided a fictitious name or 2) no name at all.)

[1] Todd Fuller is the lead author who shaped the majority of the text, conducted the interviews, gathered responses, and applied touches of embellishment. He currently works as an Associate Director for Research Development at the University of Oklahoma's Center for Research Program Development and Enrichment (CRPDE).

[2] Sonny Howell (Pawnee) is a painter, brother, uncle, uppit (grandpa), and Pawnee cultural caretaker with a BFA from Oklahoma State University.

[3] Cindy Clark, M.Ed / CRA, is a program coordinator at the University of Oklahoma's CRPDE.

[4] Marilyn Korhonen, EdD, serves as an Associate Director for Research Development at CRPDE.

[5] Apple Quick was a paternal cousin to the lead author and taught special needs kids.

[6] Nathan Miller is a maternal cousin who studies French.

[7] Ashley (Ward) McCloud is a maternal cousin with two kids and cheers on the men's basketball team at Indiana University (IU) with the same gusto as the lead author—since they both graduated from IU.

[8] Randi LeClair (Pawnee) is the lead author's wife and the granddaughter of Geraldine Howell. She is an alum of the Sundance Institute's Native Writers Lab (2010) and graduate of OU's Master of Professional Writing program (2011).

[9] Erin (Zachary) Ludwig graduated from high school with the lead author and shares an affinity for art and the Chicago Bears.

[10] Todd Petersen attended the creative writing program (PhD track) at Oklahoma State University with the lead author. He is the author of *Long After Dark* and *Rift*—both award-winning works.

[11] Lynn (Spurgeon) Kent graduated high school with the lead author.

[12] Jan Yund is a long-time family friend whose kids grew up in the same neighborhoods with the lead author.

[13] Elan Shiloh Fulman is a fictitious character.

[14] Gabe Wingfield is the web-master for the OU VPR and CRPDE. He studied religion, philosophy, literature, and post-modernism at Oklahoma State and currently plays with Anvil Salute—a frequent participant in the annual Norman Music Fest.

Off Frame / In Frame
Petalasharo, or Man Chief, was a Pawnee Indian, mythic in stature, who ended the Morning Star Ceremony during which a young woman was sacrificed.

To the Disappearance
"Kakistocracies" refer to government rule by the least qualified or most unprincipled citizens.

In Perpetuity: and Other Quandaries
U.S. Treaties: In numerous treaties between the United States and American Indian nations, the government authored agreements that

included the language "in perpetuity" to define the length of the compact and added to the dramatic flair by also including the rather purple phrase "as long as the grass shall grow and the rivers shall flow." Doing as much, the government not only forced itself into a caretaker position for that span of time, it forced many Indian nations to become, in effect, wards of the state. For its part, the government assumed (in the latter half of the nineteenth century) that most of the tribes with whom it established treaties would soon disappear or become completely assimilated into the rest of American culture—survival of the fittest, as it were. That has not been the case, however, as once decimated tribal populations have started to increase. Even today, it seems the travail of colonialism (though dressed in different attire) continues to cut its swath across the globe.

(OR, DYING AT THE WINDOW)

Pawnee / Oklahoma: In 1875, the Pawnee Nation was forcibly removed to Indian Territory in present-day Oklahoma. The Pawnees were (and are) known as the "great star gazers of the Plains," thus the reference to constellations. After removal, the tribe's population dwindled to some 600 at the turn of the century—this, after reaching 12,000 just a few decades earlier; the present tribal population is nearing 3,400.

Author Photo by Sonny Howell

Todd Fuller grew up in Indiana where he participated in the clichéd rituals of youth. Since then, he completed his Ph.D. in English from Oklahoma State University and published his first book, *60 Feet Six Inches and Other Distances from Home: the (Baseball) Life of Mose YellowHorse* (Holy Cow! Press), which was released in 2002. His poems and essays have appeared in numerous journals across the country, including the *American Indian Culture and Research Journal, American Literary Review, Apalachee Review, Barnwood Magazine, Cimarron Review, Crazyhorse, Hawai'i Review, New York Quarterly, Poet Lore, Puerto del Sol, Quarterly West, RE:AL: The Journal of Liberal Arts, Red Earth Review, South Dakota Review, Southwest American Literature, Spoon River Poetry Review, Third Coast, Weber Studies, Wicazo Sa Review,* and *William and Mary Review*. In addition, his work has also been anthologized in *The Great Plains: A Cross-Disciplinary Reader* and the *Encyclopedia of Native Americans and Sports*. In 2004, he helped found Pawnee Nation College and served as the school's first president until 2011. He currently serves as an Associate Director for Research Development at the University of Oklahoma.

SENDING HER PRAYER TO EVERYONE SHE LOVES

Cover Artist's Note: My mom, Geraldine Howell, and I went to Nebraska about four years ago. We went to an earthlodge at the Archway in Kearney, Nebraska. When she entered, she went to the fire pit and started praying. These men and Pawnee Stars are taking her prayers to everyone she loves. She passed a year or so later. Her prayers are still with us.

Cover Artist's Bio: a Full Blood Skiri (Wolf) Pawnee, from the Pawnee Nation, Sonny Howell has been fascinated with art from a young age, especially when he watched an uncle make a wolf head from clay and when he saw the art works of other Pawnee artists from the late 1950's and into the 60's when Native American art began to change with the times. While in the military, Howell attended Cameron University to study art and, after his second enlistment ended, he transferred to Oklahoma State University and graduated with a BFA in Studio Arts. His paintings are of ". . . the Myths, Legends and Exploits" of Pawnee People.

www.ingramcontent.com/pod-product-compliance
Lightning Source LLC
Chambersburg PA
CBHW020950090426
42736CB00010B/1355